SUCH STUFF AS DREAMS ARE MADE ON

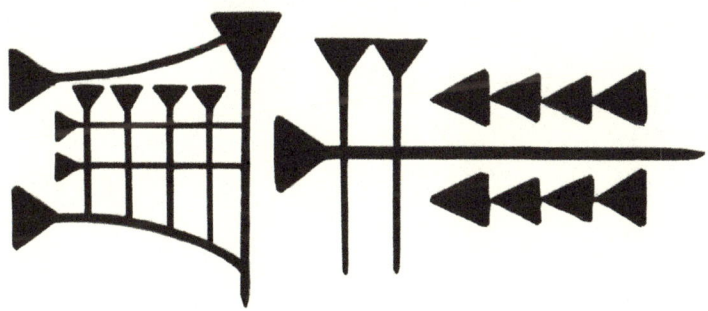

Paul Christensen

Cyberwit.net
HIG 45 Kaushambi Kunj, Kalindipuram
Allahabad - 211011 (U.P.) India
http://www.cyberwit.net
Tel: +(91) 9415091004
E-mail: info@cyberwit.net

Printed at Repro India Limited.

This book is dedicated to my late brother, Kenneth

Acknowledgements

Some of these poems were published in an earlier version. I am grateful to the following publications for bringing them out the first time.

"Haunting Old Neighborhoods," Two Men," "In Praise of Dead Mothers," in *The San Pedro River Review* (Spring/Summer 2016); "The Swimming Hole," *Bloodroot* (Spring 2016; "What I see When I Stop What I Am Doing," in *Odes and Elegies: Eco-Poetry from the Texas Gulf Coast,* ed. Katie Hoerth. Baumont, TX: Lamar University Literary Press, 2020.

Contents

Part One: Shivers of Twilight

WHAT I SEE WHEN I STOP WHAT I AM DOING

Four thousand oil rigs
suck at the Gulf's velvet skin.
The gulls fly like angels
over the glint of the iron forest.

We are burning the ancient world
of beasts, turning the dance
of life into a tongue of fire.

Out on the windless steppes
of the ocean, the pipelines
drain the ancient dreams we came from.
We are the orphans of a strange vision,
and the way forward has no map.

The highways are all we know of freedom.
Their ribbons stretch out to infinity
with cars headed for the beach,
for fun in the sun, for a chance to forget
why we toil so hard at our lives.

Who can forget childhood, with its
sandbox and shovel, the apple tree
shading us, the call of a mother
at dinner time, as if life were eternal?

Please believe me, I am giving you
a gift. It is worthless, an empty box
with its lid torn open already.
But it may be more precious than any
bank account you may have filled.
It tells you to be humble and expect nothing.

ON MY WALK THE OTHER DAY

I came upon a farm
on its last legs; the house
was leaning like an old man,
with the chimney akimbo.

I found the garden newly tilled.
The earth was dark, moist
as the human heart. Someone
who loved the smell of spring
tended it in spare moments.

How kind it seemed, this worm-
strewn, insect-jeweled patch
of seedlings and promises.

Nothing else mattered.
Not even the eroded gullies,
the wash-outs where the road
crumbled into brambles.

Let us pray, you and I,
clasping our hands together.
Let us ask for one more chance
to redeem ourselves, after
all the waste, the wars, the squandered
chances we threw behind us.

RITES OF PASSAGE

The first time I ever kissed a girl,
it was in the cemetery. She leaned
against a gravestone and put her arms
up to hold me by the shoulders.

I tasted the mold and chill of death.
But love was also there, a small power
of my awareness, a gentle, delicate
lacy breeze of roses and wild grass
that blew into me and declared I was mortal.

I heard my mother calling for me
from the back porch, under the yellow light
where I sometimes sat reading
to the hum of mosquitoes.
The house was warm and stale inside.
Her food tasted of the iron and ice
of a refrigerator, which the flames
of the stove could not eradicate.

We were prisoners of her thrift,
her worries, her narrowing consciousness
as she stood in her gray apron,
her ankles planted firmly on the stoop.
Love could not keep me in the dark forever.
My heart broke into sobs
as I tasted the salty meat, the carrots
that had stewed in the dented sauce pan.

COUNTING OUR BLESSINGS

There is a park at the end of the street
where the darkness overpowers the street lights.
The wind talks to itself, and the cracked
branches of the sycamores rattle like drum sticks.
The dead march there in the shadows,
dressed in sequins and leotards speaking
Polish and singing Slavic folksongs.
The neighbors are in their beds, necks
aching to read a book as they feel
sleep worming its way toward their heads.

We are wedged between the miracles of life
and death, in a crystal cave glinting with stars.

The city's breath has turned to fog,
festooned like cotton over the roof tops.
I hear the clamor of pans from the Chinese
restaurant; the alley is brilliant with
odors of burning fat and soy sauce.
The cats are sprawled out on the stone wall
waiting for the rattle of trash can lids.
Lonely men eat their noodles and cast
their eyes at the open door to night.

Tomorrow will come in a blaze of morning
dazzle, and the sun's bleach will linger
on the cement curbs, the parking lots,
the ordinary world in all its gold raiment.
Heaven will be hung with laundry lines

as others lean over their wicker baskets,
decorating the universe with underwear.
Such beauty in a handful of monotony,
such blessings to come from the tangy odor
of sweat being purged into a sewer.

How to see through the rust and decay
of our neglected lives, that is the riddle we ponder.

TWICE-TOLD TALES

The orchard is bare; long palsied
limbs rise and fall like ancient
ballerinas in the snow.
God has not forgotten his prohibition
against the apple. The sprung
and rusty gates of Eden
hang open to the seasons,
as if nothing ever happened.

How many devils have walked
this way on a Sunday
to eye the squandered myths
we read about. Iron-plated
clouds have fallen on the tops
of gnarly trees, their bones
rattling like saints' relics.
If the biologists are right,
none of this ever happened.

My mother leads me out
the back yard fence into the countryside.
She has watched me go blind
ever since puberty.
Ahead of us, by the smell of it,
lies springtime, and the girls
are out hanging up their linens.
They could be Eve all over again,
and here I come, tubercular and
prematurely old, a ghost
in a patched fig leaf and rotten apple.

THE CAT AND I

I saluted the flag each morning
and admired how she sunk
her tongue into the soft
billowing fur of her sex,
licking around its opening
with bored eyes, a sleepy grin.
I pored over homework, instead.

She leapt over the fence
as if it were an invitation.
The other side
of everything belonged
to the pat of her soft paws,
the slithery motion of her hips.
Her articulation of desire
scratched against the blackboard
where I did my numbers,
and learned to silence all my needs.

When old age came, she curled
in a shoe box by the bed,
her head as heavy as a rock,
her mouth used up
and wordless before death.
I never felt the cat's affinity,
not even once. It was wild,
made of all the raw things
in the world. I only ate
the cooked and severed ends.

FEBRUARY DAYS

Up in the north country
where loneliness is a religion,
women are pale as turnips
from sewing all day
at a window lit by falling snow.

Men are beer-soaked, red
in face and neck,
hands thick as oak galls in their
sleeves, full of the anger
only ice can hone.

The children grow slowly,
slick-skinned from butter
and sitting in dark corners,
their souls bright as rifle barrels
not raised since summer.

Who will gather the fuel
and feed the iron box?
The question hangs like a
pot holder in the twilight
of a kitchen.

Ice accumulates and
freezes time. A clock
ticks slowly in
the chilly hall,
whispering the news
no one will ever notice.

IN PRAISE OF DEAD MOTHERS

The wind blows through me like my mother's
voice, telling me to get up, work
harder at school, eat more rice,
brush my teeth, take a bath now and then.

She kept her eye on me, saw my flaws
the way a doctor might pore over an x-ray.
She departed this dark vale years ago,
hardly any dust remains of her footstep.
But she blows through me like a cold wind
and I am lost in my memories.

Give me five minutes at the dinette table
where she slurps tea from a chipped cup.
Give me that slice of childhood
and I'll sign over the deed to the house.
I'll willingly toss you the keys
to my Toyota truck, even fill the tank
if you're low on cash. I need the daylight
that streamed down through the window
and pooled on the linoleum floor.
I want to crawl among the legs of the table
and find my mother's slipper, put it
on her foot again. She needs my help.

A man I sometimes talk to at the gym
leans over in his towel and flips
the twenty-minute hour glass again.
You're only supposed to bake in a sauna

twenty minutes or you might suffer
some calamity of the heart. He sighs
when he sits back on the cedar bench.

He was telling me about his mother,
the fat old wretch who smoked herself
to an early death, and drank at night.
He hated her. He said he'd kill her
if she should lurch back
into his sober life. If my own mother
should grace me with her ghostly entrance,
I would sink to my knees and clutch
that stained acrylic house coat
warming her fragile bones
and keep her from escaping to the grave.

A MAN IN THE DEPTHS

I saw a man disappear into the bright sunlight
one summer afternoon. He was reassuring
himself that the world was real.
He wore an old jacket and worn-out trousers.
He gripped the handlebars with all his strength.
He was afraid of the ground and kept looking
ahead to make sure where he was going.

He didn't suspect any threat to the beauty
of the day, with its fierce light
framing him in a melancholy hour.
When his feet slipped from the pedals
and he was borne into the molten dazzle,
he hardly had time to draw his breath.
He was sure he would come back to earth,
that he had taken all the right precautions.

When his mother died the summer before,
she let her water glass fall from her hand.
He picked it up and gave it to his father,
who stood behind him.
They were spectators to a great event, a tragic
celebration of the limits of reality.
He made a note of it, and refused to mourn
the unbearable pathos of existence.
He vowed to ride his bike into the fragile
twilight, and not come back.

OLD MEN SLEEPING IN A PARK

It's always early afternoon in the park.
The traffic is slow, the heat builds
on the roofs of the surrounding houses.
Women will not venture into the iron gates
until later, when the men have wandered off.
This is a museum of junked realities,
the men having served in the war, came home
to raise families, and grew old wrinkle by wrinkle.
Their voices cracked; they had tears standing
in the corners of their eyes. Each had a pair
of eyeglasses he had worn out long ago.
Their trousers were no longer creased, but
round like stove pipes, and draped over their shoes.
They had grown shorter, fatter, their throats
were turkey-wattled; their hands fidgeted
at their frayed pockets. They swallowed slowly
and looked off to try to remember something.
Sleep came to them gently, a breeze dimming
consciousness and blinding the eyes.
They gulped when a dream opened a dead world.
They were lost in a strange city where
they had ceased to matter.
Dogs barked at the sound of a screen door slamming.
It was difficult to raise an arm, to find one's hat.
It was even harder to make out the address
of a house that might have been their own.
A boy sang in his bedroom and the sound
was like wings coming in to land from the sky.
When the phone rang in another window, no one
was there to answer it.

ELEGY FOR MY MOTHER

I smell the roses in the hospital room.
You lie there like new-fallen snow,
hardly breathing, your eyes froze over
in a state of sleep no one enters
who comes back to tell of it.

But your arms are warm, and the fingers
grasp some imaginary handshake.
Voices hang over you in dust motes,
talking gibberish about your life,
how well you look, how you will be better soon.

The roses are dead, cut off at the roots,
stranded in the cold water of a jar,
their breath still sweet before the air
turns gray around their frozen mouths,
and the sunlight turns to ammonia.

What is it like to be abandoned, to hear
the key turn in the latch and the owner
depart for the next city? How does it feel
to walk a long corridor no one uses?

A man comes to mow the lawn now and then.
He picks a day when the hours stand empty.
He has a rag in his back pocket he uses
to dab the sweat from his forehead.
How does it feel to have no money to pay him?

Death creeps up the wall and hangs from the ceiling.
It looks down at you, it waits patiently.
It is a cold shadow made of invisible silk,
and it falls over you like a bridal veil.
You are not ours any longer, but the world's.

KING OF THE BEASTS

"This is how it is," I heard my father say,
working a loose tooth at the back of his gum.
His thumb and forefinger
were buried in the saliva-silver lips.

He used to cut my hair with a barber's
scissors and a narrow comb, leaning
over me with his beer breath and soft
belly, his round face perched above
his tie like an autumn moon.

Now he picked at his mortality
with a worried look. Another tooth
gone dead, the roots withered
at the bottom of his jaw.
He chewed his food a hundred times,
especially meat, the gristly slabs
my mother fried for him each night.

He tore them like a lion in his fierce
grip, and instead of talking chose
to bury his enormous face in grease.
Famine lay at the back of his cold mind.
He would devour us if he were hungry.
My mother fed him out of fear,
while the rest of us looked on.

NEAR THE END

My father was old and feeble
when he rose from bed
to part the sick-room drapes.

Outside, the wind turned to gold
and tumbled into the empty parking lot.

He hadn't expected much,
but he could hear
the tinkling of the winter air.

When he returned to bed
he faced the side where dreams begin.

He was tired, and the earth gripped
him by his waist,
and held him in that moment without end,
and kissed him on his lips.

We are seldom alone, even close to death.
Something reminds us of the wonder we lost
and steps back into time, bringing our arms up
to dance, to hold what we could not have before.

How wonderful, he seemed to say,
before he closed his eyes.

WHERE ALL THE SEDANS ARE FIVE YEARS OLD

The men are lined up in the cafeteria,
each with a tray and a double chin,
looking around with slow, inquisitive eyes.
Their children are grown, dispersed
like chaff billowing from a combine.
The rain falls gently on the roof; only the moss
remembers anything.

If you were a heart surgeon prying up
the ribs of a heart caked with the mud
of old dinners, you would find
ghosts of first loves, panted breath
hanging from a crescent moon,
the dent in the family sedan after a night
of cowboying, as one father put it.

Such men, logy as ferry pilings,
no longer subtle or clear-thinking, sit
with stooped shoulders ready
to maneuver a cube of Jello,
the pond of gravy lying as still
as a nap in a crater of mashed potatoes.
The lawn mowers drone in the distance
as if the past were gnawing on itself.

TRAINS DON'T STOP HERE ANY MORE

I am the lover of shadows.
The twisted limbs of the elm
sag over the Odd Fellows' Hall.

Somewhere a path winds to an alley
and halts. Even the little museum
has lost its memory.

By noon teachers wrestle
with their doubts; the flag
is a limp cape waiting for some hero
riding west of here.

The music store is crammed with silent
instruments; the zither longs to be held again
in a peasant's hands.

As sunset wears down the horizon,
cracks appear in the china-blue evening.

Night lifts us gently from our names,
our clothes, and leads us back
to the wilderness to roam.

AN OCTOBER TWILIGHT

I'm reading Standard & Poor's
latest bulletin, trying to
determine whether I am
standard, or in that limbo of epithets
and rejections, simply poor.

The world's capital keeps sprouting
saplings along the trail,
turning the remaining wilderness
into rows of assets and tax havens.

I have nothing in my pockets but lint.
I am whistling past the pawnshop
where the bear sleeps, hoping
the teapot in my cupboard
has enough jingle to buy me cigarettes.

Part Two: All Rivers Meet Somewhere

ALL RIVERS MEET SOMEWHERE

A river is all there is sometimes.
A heartbeat, a way of telling time.
It carries a lot of mirrors
on its back, images of things
that cling like hexagons
on a turtle's shell. But not for long.
A river slips away from thought
without a word, and causes others
to stare and dream, and drift
downstream of their own minds.

A river talks, but no one understands.
It thinks like an old man
gathering drift wood from a storm.
There is no past to cling to very long.
All is borne seaward under
wind, accompanied by clouds.
Nothing stays that is not hard as rock.

When I walk by a river, I am not lost.
I follow its age-old course
east, for that is where the ocean lies.
The river knows that all the hills
are tilted to the sea, as if the world
were biased toward forgetting.

The river writes its watery regrets
and lets them go. It does not keep

the memory of a flood.
It has uprooted lives, and tossed
up houses as if they were mere toys.
It will not rage without a storm
to drive it wild, but when it does,
its maw gapes wide to swallow towns.
A river is all there is sometimes.

THE SWIMMING HOLE

I used to go swimming at Great Falls,
where the Potomac slows and blackens
over a deep hole. Rocks crater
there and make a rim. And eddies
indicate the scale of danger.
But who cares when a rope is limp
and you grab it with your sopping hands.
You swing free of the earth, sailing
through the chaos of the trees
hanging with white feet over an abyss.
The thrill of dying needles up your legs
as you taste vertigo on your tongue.

How rare and dignified it is to let go,
to sleep through the steep air
like a suicide already dead with fear.
Down you go, weighted like lead,
dull as fate when you know the outcome.
When the water reaches up with flabby arms
to take you to the grave, you crunch
into a ball and fight for air.
The foam surrounds you like a bed
of snow, cold to the heart, turning
your blood into an iceberg in your head.
Coming up, taking back your life
is like the first time you touched yourself,
so blind with fear, so lax with elation.

RAINING IN VERMONT

The bog spreads its oily wings
over the weeds; a sound of gulping
erupts as mud begins to melt.
A frog's eyes skim the water's edge
like an old woman praying.
I feel the knock of summer in my groin.
The heat is coming, out of the devil's pocket.
He keeps his hand against his thigh,
where all the lust of nature lies.

A cloud heaves thunder
from its bulky folds, moving toward
us with lumbering emotions.
The first watery pellets strike
the ground, parting the brush
to reveal the long, black legs of reeds.
The trance of being mortal inspires
the birds to chant their mating songs.

Toads ejaculate small croaks from
their unlettered throats; the pulse
bumps up my arm, muscles tense
like the sinews of a deer about to leap.
The horizon disappears
as grass writhes and spreads
its matted fur to the lowering sky.

THE JUNE TREES

They may be rooted to the ground, and
cannot follow me, these towers
of bark and water, sometime bird houses.
They seem solid enough until a fire.
They pose with all their dignity
in the mud, but will fall down
like everything else, in time.

Don't let such rigidity fool you.
They sweep the stars at evening, and let
the sun slip through their fingers
in the afternoon. They play soccer
with the moon, and hoist up owls
on crooked shoulders. They sing
when the wind rises, and sigh when winter comes.

They dance when no one's watching;
I've seen a willow lean down like a girl
tying her ballet shoes; and another, a
geyser of green elation, almost leave
the earth in its exuberance one windy day.
But when we're here, walking below,
you would think they took a vow of silence.

NEAR MISSES

You grow up riding a meteor across heaven.
Nothing frightens you but hesitation.
The weather parts to let you roam,
and the dark, entangled trees lean down
to caress your skin. You are the prince
of nature, its hero, promise, its rising star.

Across the street, asleep in a dim bedroom
lies the girl you love. She is a caged bird,
singing a melody so faint and uncertain
no one knows how to play it on the piano.
She rises, admires her hair, flings off
her flimsy nightgown and swims
upstream of the warm water, eager
to reach the waterfall and give in.

You are too young to grasp the situation.
You make a sandwich in the cold kitchen
and sit like a monk in the middle of silence.
You imagine a boat tied to the edge
of the lake, where you might navigate
to the silky layers of expectation,
the shivery surface of reality as it
melts into the boundless morning sky.

But you mow the lawn instead.
You steer the blade along the edges
of a flower bed, pushing against the boundary
of what is lovely and ephemeral, and

what remains of the world out in the yard.
You see her face, and her hand waves
at you, and you stand there, gazing back.
Your bones have not yet learned to dance;
your skin is sweaty, your hair hangs
in ropes of damp wilderness around your head.
Love flees the scene, riding a crow
across the tops of trees, laughing back at you.

THE FIRST OF MARCH

The birds fly overhead, liberated
from the mind. They travel wordless
over the soggy fields, eager
to find a branch to welcome them.
But the rain has fallen and nature
lies there fast asleep, unable to wake
from a dream. A coyote's thin
cry from the thicket is a warning
not to trust the world. A hawk
patrols the outer edge of forest,
keeping vigil over the corn stubble.

The birds were once the syllables
of a prayer, and voices sung them
up to the dense black clouds of winter.
Beyond lay the empty universe,
the fields of fire burning in outer space.
All along the way of flight lay the curtains
of mortality, the fallen branches
and decaying stumps of maple trees.
The road wandered away over the hills
in search of a destination.
But in this crumbling edge of time,
green shoots push through the winter cracks.

THE DEVIL'S ALMANAC

The church tower, gothic and morose,
terrifies the birds each time it tells the hour.
God's own thunder bursts from
its ancient bells, and an electric hum,
angry as a nest of hornets,
hangs in the daylight like a curse.

It's easy to dismiss the flaws of existence
You want to be carefree, to break into a dance
when the clouds part and shower you
with gold, ignite your soul with phosphor
and turn your words into a diamond mine.
You think to yourself, I'm in Paradise.

I'll fall in love around the next corner, I'll
marry money, and have bright children
who adore me. But the crows circle overhead,
and the freeway coughs with the sound
of a semi struggling up the steep hill.
I have no ambitions other than to stay alive.

I know I'm slow at catching jokes, or finding
my way through some unknown part of town.
Success keeps cleaning the skin of my friends.
They move through a universe
Einstein never dreamed of, where Newton
is the hero of gravity and Euclid builds
their houses out of perfect squares.

OUR DREAMS GROW HEAVIER

The day is devoured in the sun's jaws.
I watch the little kids milling in the cold
yard, behind a chain link fence.
They keep their eye on the dwindling
arc of light hanging over the roofs.

They sense the aging of the universe
through their gloves, their worn-down
sneakers and corduroys. The girls
collaborate on a palace in their sandbox,
with a princess looking haggard
after being scissored from a coloring book.

The world is full of strangers coming home,
alighting from stale pickups
to trudge their way up the sidewalk
into the stillness of a living room.

The wilderness lies under the peeling paint
of evening. It hardly matters that the deer
are wandering nearby, behind a thicket
of leaning birches. The owl is no more.
The geese migrated to Florida and left
behind the dusty, abandoned sky.

Love aches like a houseplant for a drink of water.
The season has scraped the glass panes
of the kitchen window until the sedans
stand in aprons of twilight like shy girls.

Each one ready to be taken out into the night
for a chance to be held, kissed on the mouth.

I find my dog in the next yard, eager
to be adopted by strangers. He follows
behind like a prisoner I captured
with sweet talk and a milk bone.
We'll weather another slice of eternity
together, under the table lamps, among
the stuffed furniture and a few memories.

America carries us on its back to the future,
and we are all anxious to be welcomed
when we get there. Look, cries a voice behind me,
the frontier is starting again. It's brand new!

THE SINGER

When I sing to myself,
I am another man,
a stranger who only comes
out of my mouth when
I am alone, sad, ready to die.

Then the voice grows
powerful, like a god's.
I could shatter a mountain
with it. I could stun an audience
that a moment before
had been talking to itself.
Now I hold it in my palm,
a wriggling mass of humanity
looking for something to believe.

It's all in the voice. Politicians
speak with it, this frightful
energy sounding the depths
of night and rising like the sun
above the skeptical, the battered.
How I love my voice. It has
wings, and I choke on its feathers
when I am merely talking.

But let me sing to my wife
and she sobs in her hands.
My children tremble
in their toddler's clothes.

My friends at work blush
at first, and then go pale
and stare at me as if I were
stepping off a sunbeam.

Sing, mighty human reed!
Bellow until the bulls run
fearful over the hill.
Split the distant stars in half
with my piercing high notes.
I am ballistic, a double-barreled
rifle pointed at the future.
I am the fountain of dreams,
the river of eternity.
I curl the Nile around my tongue
when I clear my throat.

MY NEIGHBOR'S ORCHARD

The trees across the street have shed
their apples to the ground. Green globes
bright as neon against the blue
field grass. The birds ignore them.
The neighbor cannot give them away.
He invites everyone to bring a basket,
take as many as you want, he says.

The trees are exhausted; their fruit
sucked all the juice out of them.
When it was time, the apples fell
luxuriously, like thoughts out of
an old man's memories.

They will brown soon, wasted.
They will melt away into the weeds
and disappear as easily as they came.
There are no regrets in nature.
The birds have only one emotion,
joy at the rising of the sun.
The rest is dross, hardly to be
saved or lamented over.

The arms of the trees open
and the trunks dance in the sunlight
happy to be shed of all their burdens.
"Nothing is worth keeping," they sing
over and over to the setting sun.

THE CALCULUS OF CHANGE

When you're small,
a table is the limit
of your ambition.
It stands there
out of reach,
where bread and jam
float in a hazy light
you sometimes find
in deserts, where mesas
soar and melt away
into a remoteness
too far to contemplate.

When you're grown,
too tall to grasp the edge
of a table without leaning,
the once majestic space
of hope diminishes
to a row of dinner plates
and coffee cups.
A platter smokes with chicken
and boiled potatoes,
the fruit of all you know
and work for.

Music mumbles in a bedroom,
and you know
a dreamer is at work.
She's just starting out,

on new shoes and a coat
she bought with her own money.
How brave she feels,
how magical in a dress
the color of an April morning,
her face lit by a shade
of lipstick you've never seen before.

THE MOMENT

She walked to the store
for her mother, to buy bread
and a bottle of peanut butter,
napkins for tonight's dinner.
Father was coming home, eager
to see everyone after being away so long.

The plate glass window beheld her
in that moment before she entered,
and told her she was beautiful.
She was as moved by the sight of her
long hair, her fine blue eyes,
the slenderness of her long legs
as anyone, and there were men inside
who would be eager to agree with her.

Between the corner where she stood,
the bag wobbling in her arms, her face
red with the news of her new world,
and the house that had grown small
in the minutes she was away, spread
an unexpected gulf reaching down
below her, begging her
to be a woman and escape.

POEM FOR THE TURNING WORLD

Snow stretches in lumps and knots
on the hillside, like an old bed sheet
slept on by a drunk. The sky
keeps rewriting the past with a box
of dirty light. We hold our breath
at this hour, with the new year hardly begun.
Our emotions wind around
our thoughts until they strangle us.

I stood under the trees once and dreamed
I could fly. I held out my arms and felt
my feet lift an inch from the ground.
It was enough to make the crows
fall silent over me. The wind shivered
against me, and my pants were suddenly too short.
I felt my blood turn into words
in my veins and I began to sing.

Our ignorance trembles and dissolves
as the future bullies us.
I put on my uniform and hoist up my rifle;
I am going out to meet the world.
But I hardly move a toe as I sit here
with the light draining out of the air.
God's in the kitchen making supper, heaping
platters with miracles none of us can eat.

Part Three: Life in the City

TWO MEN

Someone enters the store at closing time
and waits for service.
The twilight falls across the floor
like lava pouring from the sun.
His shoes are globes of light,
his trousers singed with embers
of the afternoon. His hands
keep altering the shadows
behind him. He has become a flame
as he stands patiently, finger
tapping on the counter, listening
intently for the sound of footsteps.

The only other living soul
is in the basement standing in the dark,
talking softly to himself.
He can't seem to sort his thoughts
and stock the heaps of unsold goods
he is responsible for. He feels
stuck in the dark, lost in it,
like a swimmer who keeps clawing
at the sea that swallows him.
He hears the man above
and cries out, but can't be heard.

HAUNTING OLD NEIGHBORHOODS

You grew up here, in the soot
of the iron mills, the blackened
doorways of a slaughter house.
A sky the color of acetylene
welds the cemetery to the horizon.
The planet is drunk and whirls
its way behind a winter sun,
kicking the moon into a pit of stars.

Clothes hang from your
narrow shoulders, your scrawny hips.
You used to dance your way home
from school, book bag for a tambourine.
Your mouth as red as a gypsy's
with the sucker balls you rolled
across your tongue. Your eyes closed
for lack of wanting anything.

Love was not yet walking by herself,
but toddling from couch to chair,
crying gibberish that could have been
your name, your destiny one day.
All that's behind you now.
Standing on your shadow, you wonder
what made all this so beautiful
it stabbed you in the heart.

ON THE BLUE ROADS

The serene composure of a barn
is lost in sleep, shoved so far back
in memory it has no daylight
of its own. It rises out of silence
like some restless ghost,
bringing to mind handfuls
of hay and the grunts of cows.

It falters at the door of attention.
There is no way to tell you
it lives still, has a life worth considering.
It has given up its place,
and lives in the ruins of fantasy.

When you open the door,
only the field presents itself.
You thought you heard a knock.
You remember some hint
of a shape standing in the yard,
but it wasn't where you looked for it.

FOUR O'CLOCK

In the living room, silence naps
like a dog. The light from outside
contracts with the coming of night.
You move to the next chair to read.

The road is empty, but it hungers
for a vision. It has no means
of pursuing its purpose.
It lies there full of expectation.

The neighbor's door is ajar.
Someone forgot to close it
when coming home. You wait
as if some unexpected miracle will emerge.

SUNNY DAYS

The sun glistens like yellow paint
on the barber shop, as if a drunk painter
dropped his bucket from a ladder
and the paint spread brightly
over the sidewalk. It's a cheerful color.

It's only in late afternoon,
after the stores close
that sidewalks turn blue,
and the gold that lined the street
turns out to be fools' gold.

The poor trudge over the moon-pale
ground dragging their children,
ignoring the peeling tar-paper roof
of heaven and the leaky rafters
full of pin-prick stars.
All night the American dream festers
in a corner of the eye, and drums
its hopes on an idle brain.

Come daybreak the orchestra
tunes up, and all remorse
evaporates with the dew.
We find the gold newly plated
on the curb, and all the common
stone repainted like Utopia.
I give three cheers to light's delusions,
and tip my old straw hat
to anyone who looks me in the eye.

WHEN THE INTRUDER COMES

When someone enters your sleep and sits
down next to your heart,
pretend no one's there, that you're dreaming.

If someone should tug at your emotions
and whisper in your sleeping ear,
do not let your pulse give you away.

If the birds should awake and it's not yet morning,
and the blue sky tears itself free
of the stars, refrain from shouting.

Good things come to the modest,
the deserving, the deniers of selfishness,
the shy ones, the less-than-eager ones,

while the rest of us who lunge at life
and pray for an intruder, suffer
most and laugh the loudest.

TRAFFIC JAM

Summer had hurt us like a hammer
all through July, and crushed
our spirits in August. We were limp.
We hated heat. It entered us like
swamp gas, and poisoned our noses
to smell its rotten fertility.

She fanned herself with a magazine,
red-faced, annoyed at everything.
The gray grass sagged on brittle
stems; the wind teased the bees
and sent them spiraling out of flowers
into the angry sky. Mountains were
caked in brown dust, like elephants.

To breathe was to pull ten pounds
of iron into your throat, and spit it out again.
A car inched forward
as dark and greasy as a burn
from a pan of bacon. Nothing stirred
for the next half hour, as we sat
there staring straight ahead like
murderers on trial. All of us guilty.

WHAT I LEARNED BY GOING ABROAD

Too many barrels of wine turn bad
in the cellars below Gigondas.
There are not enough mouths to swallow
the ruby liquor in a hefty goblet
or finish the *foie gras* before closing time.
The telephone rings and a duchess
begs for a *rendez-vous*, but I'm running late.

My check from the lottery goes uncashed.
It's a shame the poor live day to day
in the gloom of a one-room tenement
on the sour, crumbling edge of town.

Nations die in the cities; rigor mortis
sets in where farms spread out their weedy
fields to dry. I've seen children who look older
than their parents from sleepless nights.

It's time to walk the dog, but there is no dog.
He ran off with a drug dealer and never looked back.
The moon lost one of its phases and hangs
from the night like a broken street lamp.

One of these days I'm going to feast on
pintade smothered in morels and chestnuts.
I'll ask the waiter to open the Petrus and drown
me in elation, while the millionaires look on.

THE CONSOLATIONS OF AUTUMN

The maples disrobe
in the drained light. It's October,
and summer's dust whirls
above a green combine
as it eats a corn field, spewing out
ode after ode to love.

Crows carry a magician's
cape and hang it on the moon.

What we know collapses
into a swarm of gnats,
a hum of reconsiderations.
No one regrets what we hoped
about the future; it's just that
we are there now and it disappoints us.

The moon is a sliver of ice
lodged like a wisdom tooth in the dark.

There are households we cannot see,
mud shelters under the grass
where nuts are piled,
and tiny grains lie hoarded
for when the ice steals our breath.
Time gnaws on the heart.

Everything green turns to red;
what cannot burn drowns in yellow pools.

THE WEATHER REPORT

Old snow packs up like bad habits against
the house. Rigid as arthritis, like
fat hanging from the dark side of the body.
It has no further use; it has fallen, and lies
there dead, a stiff soldier still clutching
an empty rifle. I hear the dogs far off.

The sky lies in ruins, a landfill of exhausted
dreams strewn over the hollows of space.
The air hardly moves. The music we ache
to hear has slowed and turned to ice
in the river beds. The children look old
in their heavy coats, their muddy boots.

I smell soup in the kitchen, last night's
echo of hope and anticipation. The dark
keeps arranging its shape under the table,
like a restless drunk trying to sleep.
The west grows feeble as night comes,
a light flickering above an abandoned church.

NIOBE'S TEARS ARE ON MY I PHONE

The cigars are displayed in a museum
just outside Nashville. Music plays
from a tinny speaker in the driveway;
aging teenagers congregate on the loading dock.

The sun is hot today; it is hot every day.
The boys snag flies with their clenched palms
while the girls watch, attentively, chewing gum.
I am moved to tears by their intensity.

The entire universe is invisible overhead.
Only the moon hangs loose like a button
someone forgot to push through the eye of a vest.
A senator moves slowly toward the baseball field,

panting with exertion. His briefcase is empty.
His eyes dart left and right, as if alert
to any political shift in the wind.
He is homesick for a bottle of gin and a hotel room.

May the ancient gods forgive us for what we have made
of this great continent. It lies there deep in thought
between earthquakes, in the arms of a hurricane
that never found its way to Oklahoma.

THE NEON QUEEN OF SCIENCE

Madame Curie's fingers lie there
in a crypt of the Pantheon like Christmas lights,
glowing in their residues of radium.
She is more eerie than a saint,
her rotting hands lying primly together
in prayer, her dress faded
under the leaden dust of a century.
I press my face against the tomb
until a custodian brushes me away.

All night she dipped those fingers
into the vats of divine blood,
and felt the secrets of a mythical world
caress her skin, and leave eddies
of white smoke. She was addicted to radiance
and clutched at it like Saint Catherine of Siena.
Nothing could feed her soul
but this alchemical fulguration bubbling
in the tubs, while her husband fussed
with the strings of his rubber apron.

Even her cookbook is radiant, filled
with the alchemical notes of an epicure.
Her Nobel diplomas hang in the dark
of a stone niche, and the keys to her institutes
dangle from a hook near the door.
Chopin's *mazurkas* tinkle on a loop tape
in the lobby, like the chattering
teeth of ghosts. Everything smells like snow,

and when the sun penetrates the armor
of the sky, at around ten in the morning,
the ground glitters with cold fire.

IN THE BOGS OF TIME

They're boarding up my old neighborhood
and shipping it South, to the memory dump
where the Civil War lies buried.
I hear the saws, the rapping of hammers
against the roof beams, the shuffle
of laborers coming and going along
wooden ramps. The vans arrive and drag
away my childhood fantasies. I see my shorts
flying from a lamp post like the flag
of a dead country. I weep for my lost dimension.

Out on the lowland swamps of Mississippi,
where the embers of racism still smoke
and glow, the Civil War sinks into the fertile
muck of an old tobacco field. The bloody
planks of a fort jut up out of the weeds
like the prow of a sinking ship, with
the cries of the wounded still whimpering
in the heat of the afternoon. I pity them.

General Lee wanders the perimeters
and observes the mystique of decay.
He had lowered the height of southern men
by an inch or two, and joined the ranks
of Napoleon and Julius Caesar, Stalin
and Mao, Pol Pot and other heroes of destruction.
He reads from his prayer book with his
visor pulled down, just as the first
vans arrive to deposit the driftwood of my estate.

Just like the tree that's planted by the waters
I shall not be moved . . .
Though all Hell assail me, I shall not be moved.

WHERE THE TRUTH ENDS

A liar
is an acrobat
tumbling through
the air beyond the truth.

He breathes the unlived
words with ease, and moves
with the grace of an imaginary
animal, scaling the lower
mounds of rock
in long thin leaps.

Gravity will not cling to him.
His hair hangs from his scalp
like someone else's conscience.
He eyes possibilities
as he talks, choosing
among the veins of reality
that gather like a spider's web.

He wags his tongue like Orpheus
who charmed Cerberus once,
and raised each head until it bit
the void and called it food.
Hades looked on in wonder,
scratching his filthy beard.

Every lie begins in outer space,
among the airless planets

where nothing grows. The dust rises
with his breath as he tells us
what we can't believe,
but beg to, anyway.

A PORTRAIT IN BARS OF IVORY SOAP

Hatred wears a mask
and talks piety
through his loose dentures.
Your stomach turns
to smell his breath.
You know he is from
out of town, but where?
His sister lives in a long shadow
near a bridge and cries
at her window.
He visits her and brings
stale bread. He has no friends.
He is full of suspicion,
and shares it with strangers.
He was married once, but no one
can remember to whom, or what.
He believes in malice, broken
promises, drunken confessions,
in closing down the government.
He hangs around the courthouse
hoping to catch sight of the condemned.
You think you don't know him.
But he's been to your table,
eyed your daughter, your wife,
your garage full of extra tools.
He will try to implicate you
in some scandal, so be ready for him.

MODERN TIMES

These are the days when every leader
is either bow-legged or hump-backed,
and who tells us he is perfectly normal.

We who need a savior believe him
when he shows us how pretty he is.
He has a picture of himself next to the dais.

I'm the first to leap to my feet and applaud.
I love the free-fall make believe gives me
in a world without substance.

Look at all the sad trees in the forest,
how they mope in their heavy green suits,
how they refuse to dance with the wind.

My wife tells me I've been left behind;
all my friends are rich and famous,
and live in mansions above the river.

Not so, I shout over dinner. I have pierced
the gray sky to let my eyes peek into heaven,
and I envy no one. Not even God.

HAPPINESS IS NEVER IN YOUR POCKET

I roamed around in the tunnels
below Philadelphia, with my older brother.
Guiding us was an old construction
lantern we stole from a work site.
The black air led us into the heart
of the city, with its throbs reverberating
against the tiled walls. The Delaware
was below us, down endless ramps
of whispering sewer water, where
tug boats gunned their diesels
pulling a line of garbage scows
out to sea. You heard the echoing voices
of another world, from a graveyard,
from people waiting over a storm grate
to catch a bus. The rain turned the world
into a mesh of pulses and static,
and we felt the cold wind against us.
If God exists, he presides over an immaculate
heaven of red carpets, low-hanging brass
lamps. The angels sing to him from aloft.
The sky spreads out at his feet
like so much snow drifting up against
the gold-painted gates to his kingdom.
Down here, the dark is edible; we feel
it slither through our lips into our lungs.
There is no evil, just this aching desire
for light, when noon disintegrates.

THE FUTURE IS LYING TO US

The city is ruled by dragons
with bright yellow mouths and
sharp teeth; they move laboriously
over the rubble of abandoned myths.
The past is as fine as ash
and even the homeless have gone
to the countryside to live.

The city can't speak; its only
word is a car alarm wailing
behind a liquor store.
The city's ghosts are moving
to Mexico to join the parades
on the day of the dead. No one else
remembers who they were.

The city is rising higher and higher
over the dying wilderness.
Its apartments are hanging from the stars.
The rich are borne on the bosoms
of gold-painted elevators to dine
with bald eagles, who wear Rolex watches.

Everyone reads the New York *Times*
over breakfast, and *Style* magazine
on Sunday. The boys who model for
Ralph Lauren weigh eighty pounds
in their sleek high-water slacks.
The women are as frail as Pre-Raphaelite angels
and have forgotten how to smile.

THE SOBBING OF ALARM CLOCKS

My father saw a man float out of his bedroom window
and into his neighbor's house. He was asleep.
He had dreamed his way down to the bottom
of memory, and where he felt the fine
crumbs of sand at the bottom of his soul,
he dug a little further and disappeared.

It's why children dig at the beach, bringing
up shovels full of wet gray sand. They know where
the heavens begin, at the back door of reason.

The long gray slab of ocean that limits our
progress on the land is a reminder that we know
so little about our lives. The milky, sudsy
moodiness of water houses great wonders
like the secretive giant squid, whose suction-studded
tentacles trail behind forty and fifty feet
as they fly through the salty darkness.

Sometimes, the giant squid enters my neighbor's window
and hangs above the bed where he sleeps.
He wakes in the morning tasting brine on his lips.
He drives to work unwilling to be a drudge,
but the laws of cruelty and cunning that rule
over the city are stronger than imagination,
hence the despair we surrender to night.

AN ELEGY

When my brother died after a long illness,
my father went through his belongings
and found a pair of shoes he liked.
He put them on and you could tell they were
too small, too narrow for his wide feet.
He wore them anyway, for "yard work,"
I think he said. Thrift was the rule,
a sterner law than grief.

That's why the poor suffer in America.
The dark streets with their brown hedges,
the sagging fences, the busted mailboxes,
the taped windows, the kids crying
in the dreary back bedroom while their mother
looks on without any emotions left,
all this adds up to a hallway painted
in brown enamel, shattered by the jarring
slashes of graffiti. My father walks
in the graveyard with his squeaky shoes,
and the ghosts listen. The silence is full
of possibilities he never thought about.

WHAT I'VE HEARD ABOUT
PHILOSOPHY

I haven't seen my neighbor in months.
I heard rumors she had died.
But there she is, in her window,
pale as a lamp in a lonely room,
her hair pulled tight behind her head.

She used to laugh a lot, a spirited woman.
She may have loved a man too much.
I'm told her children moved to Mexico
to be near the sun; they never write to her.
A dog hangs about the house like a beggar.
A bowl of water looks fresh enough.

I'm probably better off. She has no money
left; the car in the garage has turned to stone.
America towers over us in all its brilliance,
a living proof of liberty, the freedom
to escape from care and soar like Icarus.

SORTING THROUGH MY THINGS

The silence keeps gathering time
in its hands, molding it into figures
I partly recognize before they vanish.
Others meditate, but I spend my time
squinting at the empty corner
trying to read a newspaper without words.
Things happen and people rush around
worrying the world will end;
but I stay seated with my feet resting
on an ottoman, in my bathrobe and slippers,
my hair ballooning out of my scalp
like the black soot from a New Delhi restaurant.

It's prematurely night where I live,
each afternoon lopped off with a butcher knife
to make way for the darkness.
I'm not afraid anymore. My childhood
is used up and lies there in the past
like a crumpled love letter I never finished.
Even the furniture has a certain sour
smell to it, as if I had bought reality
from a thrift store. I rise to wash the dishes
only to discover I haven't eaten anything.
Perhaps I should stay home once in a while
to get to know myself, to break the ice
with a soul I haven't spoken to in ages.

THE DIARY OF A FOOL

My soul has never spoken to my heart.
They are like feuding siblings
in the back seat on a long car trip.
One will get the bed by the window
when we stop for the night;
it knows to bolt from the car
and race behind my father
up the stairs of the guest house
and flop down with triumphant ownership.

I take the bed in the cold corner.
I eat the last piece of bacon, the one
that is soft and undercooked, and poke
the egg left in the pan too long.
I feel my soul laughing behind me,
in that part of attention that lacks words.
Wisdom is the black dog without a leash,
who knows where home is and takes
the turn into the dark, certain of what lies
beyond the last street sign.

Someone took the wilderness out of me,
and gave me short pants and a t-shirt.
I was told life was full of terrors, and that
a peanut butter sandwich would shield me.
When I felt the nausea of death grip me
by the waist and shake me, I had a candy bar
in my pocket to console me.
And when the devil whispered to me

and my eye gazed at the lawless perfection
of a girl's face, I was late for dinner.

I saw spring come and go in the windows
and never felt the pull of earth.
My feet jumped over the sidewalk cracks
to avoid the worst, but the path led
to an alley where fate hung its damp laundry
and the weight of reason made the sky
sag overhead. I am only human, and ask
the creaking, rusty universe to forgive me.

Made in the USA
Las Vegas, NV
25 June 2021